A Man of Breeding

OrangeBooks Publication

1st Floor, Rajhans Arcade, Mall Road, Kohka, Bhilai, Chhattisgarh 490020
Website: **www.orangebooks.in**

First Edition, 2026

ISBN: 978-93-7426-614-4

Price: Rs. 210.00

Printed in India

A MAN OF BREEDING

TALENT IS ALWAYS HIDDEN; NOT THAT IT IS NOT EXISTENT. SPOT IT AND NURTURE IT PROPERLY" - MOHAMMED ILYAS BABAR.

MARYAM BABAR

OrangeBooks Publication

www.orangebooks.in

Index

Introduction

I was in my teens I remember when people around me used to narrate anecdotes of my grandfather. Besides, I was also being told that I used to have a friendly relationship with him. I always try to recollect my childhood memories but in the end I come up with my 'think tank' as nothing.

A deep thought and courage from my dearest parents persuaded me to narrate you what is known to me. I felt that the contributions of such a man to Indian athletics should not be neglected, and like other victorious sports stars of today, he should also be presented to you.

It did not take much time for my thoughts to become action. The knowledge given by others, and the effort of mine today, culminated in 'A Man of Breeding.'

'A Man of Breeding' is not only a concise biography of my grandfather, who was an enigmatic personality and a persuasive athletic coach, but also includes the elements of his life that explain the quality of good social behaviour. It describes how grandpa's life was dominated by his uncompromising faith. Though not with us anymore, he has left his footsteps in the sands of time for others to follow.

Well, I am not a writer but a science student who is pursuing clinical nutrition. I was in the ninth standard when I wrote the first draft of this book, and I never thought it would take years for me to reach its final edition.

Although the upcoming pages are the reflection of my mind, and I may forget a scene from it, a location or simply an important date if someone asks. But the common thing that exists in every chapter of this book is 'zindagi mein saadgi apnao, jitni saadah tumhari zindagi hogi utni pareshaniyan kam hogi.' Surely, it tends to leave an impact on you as well.

I felt that if even one reader of this book finds my work inspirational, then the endeavour to write this book will be well worth it. It will make me contented. I hope you will not dissatisfy giving your valuable time and reading it patiently. Hence, this book is for you, dear readers.

- *Maryam Babar*

October, 2019

Hyderabad, India

Let Passion Endure and Carve the Path of Destiny

The 'stone city' Gulbarga also called 'Kalaburagi' is in the Indian state of Karnataka, India. It is a popular historical town of today which is known for its cultural heritage and temples. The progenitors of my grandpa were the natives of Gulbarga. The grandfather of my grandpa, Mr Abdul Qader sahab, was a government employee. He had two children: Ruqaiya Begum (Babar's mother) and Abdul Aziz (Babar's uncle). The mother of my grandpa was a down-to-earth and pious woman. She got married in Gulbarga to Mr. Mohammed Ahmed Khan, who was a lawyer. My grandpa was in his mother's womb when she wanted separation from her husband. Very soon, in a span of two years, they separated. It was during these hard times that my grandfather, Mohammed Ilyas Moizuddin Khan Babar, opened his eyes in Kalaburagi on 2nd February' 1926. Though my grandpa belonged to the 'Khans,' he never used this name officially. My grandpa's mother named him 'Babar' as she believed that grandpa was as brave as the Mughal emperor Babar. Hence, grandpa was popularly called 'Babar.'

My grandpa's mother took teacher's training and started to earn for her child. Although her father doesn't want her to work, she insisted and said, 'You did my marriage, but it is my destiny that it was not successful. My child and I are not a burden on anyone.' With this strategy, she overcomes the hard times of her life. She was employed under the government service and was transferred to Aurangabad, Vijapur, Osmanabad, Latur, and Kandar. No matter wherever she travels, she is always accompanied by her dear son. Anyway, she fought an uphill battle. Worshipping God with a pure heart and seeking help for her child was her only motto. She used to pray, 'Oh God, if this child, after growing up, is going to become pious, keep him in this world or just pick him, I will be patient.'

My grandpa was two or three years old when his mother permanently settled in Hyderabad. Initially, they found space in Nampally Tekh masjid, but later they moved to Red Hills. It was a nice place with a good society and cooperative people. Anything taught by his mother used to be an indelible mark for my grandpa. He used to obey his elders and learn what was right and wrong under their guidance. In his growing years, he used to follow a very systematic routine to maintain his healthy habits always. Playing outdoor games was his best hobby. He would play as if he risked his life and limb. Though he would always play less and injure himself more, it was never a halt in his game. Whenever he returned home wounded, he would be badly scolded. The scars of his sports mania were seen till his death.

It is said that a mother's lap is the first school. For all those religious people and prophets born earlier, the same mother's lap trained them, but nowadays people understand it as little as possible. When grandpa was in school, he used to go along with his mother. He was a notorious lad. Studies never became the priority of Grandpa throughout his academics. Playing games and satisfying oneself was his sole desire. He acquired primary level education from different schools and cleared his secondary school exam from Anwar ul uloom.

Even though he was brought up by a single parent, his mother never allowed him to feel this emptiness. He was brought up among the wise teachings of his mother, grandfather and uncle, which made him into a positive person. His mother bravely took all the tussles of his life on her back since his birth.

After clean blackboards and teary eyes, now's the time to get into the college life. As I'm experiencing it is the most exploring and implementing stage in the life of every student. He took admission in City College of Arts and Science and chose commerce to read. During this period, there was a shortage of oil. In Red Hills, near my grandpa's house, all his friends rented a room for group study. Everybody used to gather there at a specific time and study. Teamwork really enhances our knowledge and improves our capacity to study. Everything was going well except the lantern. It used to give very dim light because there was less oil. For the sake of approximately twenty students' education, my grandpa's mother asked her nephew to fetch palm oil from Gulbarga at her expense. At that time, exporting palm oil from Gulbarga was banned. But one always has options to get one's work done. People used to buy a vegetable seller's a cane basket, put the oil box in it and spread vegetables over it. Then this basket would be carried to Hyderabad. In this way, she always tried her best so that her son's education wouldn't be spoiled. But her son would read only sports books hidden inside his subject books in front of his mother as well as his teacher. He would order 'World Magazine' from London and was a regular buyer of it. He used to order magazines from

Germany as well. It was a dream of his mother that one day her son would complete his graduation with good marks, wear the black gown and click a picture in it. But the son, being indulged in his 'craze for games,' used to fail. Even to write his supplementary exam, he would fool his mother and spend his exam fee on buying his sports stuff.

The young, zealous grandpa used to look like a tall, straight pole, exhibiting a perfect athlete's look. With a roughly mechanised schedule in his mind, he would wake up early in the morning and rush to his college. He would sit with his friends and absorb a lot of knowledge, which inspired him to bulk up his biceps and triceps. Eventually, after a session of rigorous practice of his game in Secunderabad, my grandpa used to sluggishly reach home with heavy steps. In the evening, as soon as he stepped into the house, his grandfather would shout, 'You're wasting your entire mother's income on games!' After a good tongue-lashing, he would go and calmly hide his cups and medals in the showcase. He used to share his showcase with his cousin (his uncle's daughter). Her name was Mumtaz. They used to quarrel a lot over their belongings in it. Even for other things, they used to argue so much. When my grandpa's grandfather became a little angrier with him, the cousin who was winding up the situation would say, 'Look, grandpa, only in vain has he accumulated so much.' On hearing this, my grandpa would get a bonus scolding. One day, my grandpa got fed up with these frequent fights. Gnashing his teeth, he threw all his cups and medals in an old well in the public garden at Nampally.

He never brought any cup or medal he had won to his house after that; instead, he gave it to his friends.

From 1950 to 1957, he was the state champion of Hyderabad in the 110-meter hurdles and the high jump. He also represented the state in national games in 1952 and 1955. He also used to play badminton in college. Once for a badminton competition, he went to Sri Lanka as well. He didn’t take a single penny from anyone at his house. He borrowed some money from his friends and went for about a week or fifteen days. At that time, my grandpa was on the cusp of his career. He didn’t hire any coach to get training, nor did he ever speak of his desire to anyone. He was paddling his own canoe. Only by reading books and practising daily, he began guiding others at the same time. Very soon, he gained popularity in the army for his unique skills and great enthusiasm. It didn't take long for him to get his first assignment, which was to train young soldiers at the Artillery Centre in Hyderabad. A military car or a truck used to pick and drop him off daily. His chicken-hearted grandfather became terrified of the military man with the massive car who arrived at his door every day. But his grandson consoled him, saying, ‘There's no need to be afraid, grandpa; I'm training soldiers in the army for a short time.’ The old man replied, ‘You have already caught yourself playing games; now what does it mean to teach others?’ ‘I will get the license,’ Grandpa added. Well, after a month, his hard work yielded positive results. He was paid Rs. 300 for training the soldiers each month. The first income was placed in the blessed hands of the oldest in the family. His grandfather, surprisingly, anxiously asked where and how he earned this money. 'From the same, sports grandpa,' the young man replied. Overwhelmed with happiness, the old man replied, 'The game also happens to be like, if we teach others, we get money.' Although very surprised, he blessed his grandson and wished him good luck.

Looking at the maturity of his dearest grandson, he gave up frequently scolding him; rather, they were all replaced by blessings. To see his dearest grandson fulfilling all his responsibilities was the last chapter of his life. 'My boy has turned into a good and responsible man; now he is earning money too; don't you worry, daughter!' Your efforts have been rewarded. These were the last words spoken by Mr Mohammed Abdul Qader Sahab in his last moments.

Earn with Wisdom and Bestow with Grace

We know athletics is a competitive field of sports involving running, walking, jumping, etc. Track and field, cross-country running, marathon, pole vault, steeple chase, and hurdles are some of its competitions. For non-sportspeople like me, it's just a sport that I happen to watch on TV just to see what I know about it. But for the sports stars, it is all about hard work and good results. For Mohammed Ilyas Babar, athletics was both his hobby and profession. Let me explain the essence of coaching in the words of my legendary grandfather. "I view coaching as an art to do it, you must be passionate about it. It should not be a job. It must come from within you, and you must enjoy it and not do it as a mere job that pays for your livelihood. What it does so is incidental. But the most important thing is that it should be both your hobby and your first love. It is like painting or music. Maybe that's why I don't get bored with it or have felt bad about getting awards and honours for it."

Grandpa's coaching career began at the university level. On the stimulation of Mr Ghouse Mohammed Khan, the outstanding tennis player, Grandpa trained many athletes in 1956. One of them was B.V. Satyanarayan, who represented India at the Rome and Tokyo Olympics. Illustrious players like Saroja Goplan, Nausha Thandwala, Aziz, and Mr P.K. Mahanand, who was also a good friend of my grandfather, were university and state champions in discuss throw and shot put. He went on to become a national weightlifting champion and a wing commander in the Indian Air Force. Besides, the coach also instructed Maqbool Ahmed, who made history in the inter-university championship by winning gold in the 500, 1500, and 10,000-meter races and winning the individual "Best Athlete" trophy in four inter-varsity meets.

Grandpa’s obsession with his game was increasing with every passing day. His distinguished training and polished skills attracted people. In the year 1958, he was called to the National Defence Academy, Khadakvasla, Poona, to train officer-cadets. The majority of his pupils here were brigadiers, majors and generals who used to respect grandpa as their guru despite their high ranking. The following year, he got the opportunity to work at his most lovable place, the Rajputana Rifles Regimental Centre (RRRC). Consequently, he left for Fatehgarh. In Fatehgarh, very soon, he made a friendship with a Hyderabadi family who owned a huge Koti ‘Gulzar.’ People here were all Shia Muslims. Grandpa allotted a room to an aged man from his part of Koti without any rent. That pious man used to pray all night. When granny used to visit grandpa, that old man used to monitor granny in grandpa’s absence.

When a runner used to submit himself to my grandpa’s firm and challenging training schedule, he was bound to do well at both the national and international levels. Although he was a hurdler himself in his time, he coached sprinters, hurdlers, steeplechasers, marathon runners, and mostly distance runners. On the field, he was habituated to training the soldiers on sand. Round-the - clock soldiers rigorously practised my grandfather's most difficult techniques, which were not a child’s play. The soldiers were sometimes fed up with the constant training and striving for such long hours. If anyone used to glance at the soldiers practising on the field, they would feel pity for them. But the happiness of soldiers will know no bounds when they come out with flying colours.

Many coaches influenced my grandfather's training philosophy. The way Percy Cerutti trained Herb Elliott was always appreciated by him. He admired the techniques of Franz Stampfl, who coached Roger Bannista and Chataway. He used to say that his union with the late Jayanti Rousseau was helpful. My grandpa was inspired by Lucknow Christian College as well. He was a superb coach and a very good teacher. Dr Otto Peltzer was a German world record holder and was considered a "goldmine of information" by grandpa. My grandfather used to admire his dedication towards his work when Mr Peltzer was jobless and was starving severely. Dr Otto Peltzer's training methods, knowledge of physiology, psychology, and diet were also beneficial for him. After gaining a prolonged education in the training philosophies of great coaches, Grandpa drew up his own methodology. He kept in mind the Indian environment, diet, facilities provided, and, of course, the average build of athletes. Everything is about teaching the basics, and the significance of hard work and dedication was his priority. Undoubtedly, there are other advanced approaches in coaching, but everything revolves around the common features like speed, endurance, and physical conditioning that he strategised.

Among his pupils was a marathon runner called Jagmal Singh. As far as I know, he was forty or forty - two years old. Though he was not eligible to compete with the young blossoms, he still represented India in the 1960

Olympic Games in Rome, Italy. He clocked his distinctive best and became the first Indian to run the distance in two hours. The graph of his stars started with Jagmal Singh, Joginder Singh, who was a shot-put runner, Makhan Singh, who won gold in the relay, and Tarlok Singh. Though the latter was not confident enough about his game. But the master motivator pushed him with positivity and saw him performing well. Grandpa never coached any athlete unless he could totally rely on him. He used to say, 'Motivation is the prime factor of success. Training is not just good enough. There must be some comprehension between a coach and an athlete.' Grandpa had always run the extra mile for his trainees. Even though grandpa was a person of few words, he created an approachable and easy-going personality towards his pupils. It is not a mere saying, but he actually meant it. One of the pupils of grandpa was mentally disturbed. Her parents were separated and even wanted to divorce. Grandpa spoke to her parents and tried his best to clear their misunderstandings. His effective wisdom made his pupil's parents reunite. Till today, his pupil is very grateful to grandpa and always expresses her gratitude whenever she calls granny.

In 1961, foreign athletic coaches arrived in India to train Indian coaches. To obtain a diploma within 6 months from NIS Patiala, Indian coaches Ken Bosen, CM Muthiah, JS Saini, and Jagmohan Singh joined the 1st batch. My grandfather also joined the batch to gain additional excellence and qualifications. Foreign coaches left when the training was over, and in their place the Indian coaches of batch 1 were appointed to train the upcoming batches. But grandpa declined this offer because he simply had a tuning and would only do a custom job, and returned to Fatehgarh.

On one chilly night of winter, my grandpa went to Farrukhabad, which is on the outskirts of Fatehgarh. He went to meet his friend Mr Daniel, who was a Christian. My grandpa had a sincere companionship with his friend. He spend a quality time with his friend and after a couple of hours at around 11 pm, grandpa decided to go back home. Grandpa has a habit of asking the driver's name whenever he sits in a ride. He would casually talk to the driver, ask family details and humbly give whatever he had in his pocket after reaching his destination with a grimace. On that night, he took off his jacket and put it in on the driver. 'I am not cold, you put it on, sir,' the driver requested. Grandpa ignored. With intense communication, half an hour passed, and grandpa reached his home after a long route. He paid the fare and went to the drawing room inside his house.

He took off all his clothes and shoes and gave them to the auto rickshaw driver. Granny was amazed to see Grandpa's appearance when he entered the house. Grandpa pacified her and said that the driver was poor, so he helped him. Granny intelligently said, 'You would have taken out clothes from your closet and given him.' But grandpa feared that he would lose a chance to do a good deed if the driver rushed away. Grandpa's mother always knew this extreme level of his son's generosity. Therefore, she always used to warn Granny, 'Mumtaz, you will see that one day Babar will donate his worn clothes to someone.' That night, the prediction of a pious mother became true.

After completing his contract in Fatehgarh, grandpa returned to Hyderabad in 1964 and found employment at the Electronic and Mechanical Engineering (EME) Centre in Secunderabad. From Red Hills to Bularam, he used to go by bicycle. Later, a car was arranged for his pick-up and drop-off. He would leave after Fajr prayer, and sometimes even before that. In Bularam, he was allotted a house to stay in during his working hours. He would begin his training as soon as he arrived on the field. While the soldiers used to run, he would be with them on a bicycle. Around eleven o'clock, after the morning session of training, he used to have breakfast. Followed by heavy training till evening, he would reach home and perform the Isha prayer. He used to be extremely tired.

My grandmother used to take his shoes off. His legs and feet would be swollen from paddling a bicycle for such a long route. Lifting his hand to take morsels of food would sometimes be a burden for him. In that case, Granny used to make small morsels and put them in his mouth. She used to sometimes say, ‘Oh God, don’t ever give a sportsman as a husband to any girl.’ This was the level of his hard work everywhere. *“Results cannot be immediate. Training must be planned in such a manner that results are sustained even if they are late,"* he used to confidently say. In the EME centre, foremost among his pupils were Shirke, a national sprint champion, and B.S. Barua. He turned Barua into an Asian champion within three years. Barua won the 800 meters in 1 minute, 49.4 seconds at the Asian Games in Bangkok in 1966. He used to publicly say, ‘Without Babar, I could have achieved nothing.’

Fearless Hearts Weave the Tapestry of True Friendship

Delhi, other than the union territory of India, the capital of India, the second wealthiest city of India, the center of the national capital region, the largest commercial center in northern India, the twenty-eighth most visited city in the world, one of the fastest growing cities in the world, the city of rallies, was always remembered and called by my grandpa as *"dilli dilwaloun ki."* He used to love the city, the people who lived there, and, foremost, his favourite, The Nizamuddin Markaz.

The ever-smiling coach was happy again to work in the Rajputana Rifles Regimental centre and to live among the brave army soldiers. It was 1967 when he congregated as a coach with the army to feel and breathe patriotism. He had a special feeling for the athletes in the army. *'Though I was never in the army, I always felt close to it. I was with the services during all the wars, and I saw how hard they worked,'* he vindicated. In the army, athletes would be eager and hungry to do well, he observed. Sometimes he would make them do three workouts if necessary. Others outside would be unable to do so, he pointed out.

As always, rising with the sun was one of his regular habits. After a leisurely and enjoyable light breakfast with 2-3 cups of hot milk tea, he would then leave for his morning training session. At ten or around eleven o'clock, he would return to take a breath and have his mid-morning meal. Until the call of afternoon prayer, he would be asleep. Very rarely, he would be at home during his late afternoon prayers, or else he would be seen on the field for his second session of training. He used to spread a *janamaz* (a prayer mat) on the field itself to perform his prayer if needed. Finally, he would reach home in the evening.

At times, after taking a power nap after a morning session of training, he would walk towards the barracks. He would check whether all his athletes were provided with good provisions and whether they could meet their requirements. If everybody were gumming regularly and properly? Whether everyone got a good diet or not, he would keep an eye on everything. He was an uncompromising diet planner. He would make sure his athletes were provided with a wholesome diet of vegetables, chapattis, pulses, and eggs—in short, a square meal. Without fail, he would make use of pure honey, jaggery, and desi ghee during the training. He would even ask the soldiers to fetch desi ghee from their villages. Also, his athletes' diets would be supplemented with multi-vitamins and vitamins C and E to help them heal from pains and injuries. He never used drugs and never recommended them to his students. He believed that drug use was not only dangerous but also immoral. If ever he found any deficiency in the above things, he would demand it from the sports agency or ask the soldiers to spend their own money on it. But two glasses of fruit juice were equal to half of their monthly salary. For those athletes who couldn't even afford a balanced diet, he would spend his money to fill their stomachs and satisfy their appetite. He always wished to provide a better diet for his pupils, but financially it was not possible, though he tried his best. His small and hard-earned money were sufficient to fulfil the basic needs of his huge family and even to help other needy people.

His trainees include Shri Ram Singh, Shivanth Singh, Ratan Singh, Jagbir Singh, and Geeta Zutshi, and the list continues. Shri Ram Singh Shekhawat, on the other hand, was Grandpa's star pupil. He was a Rajput. He was his most conscientious and obedient student. He used to be a fearless competitor for his future generations. He never complained that he was tired or wanted to reschedule his routine. He won the services title in the 400 m in 1967, the national title in the 800 m in 1968, and the silver medal in the Asian Games in 1970, breaking B.S. Barua's record. He used to say, *'I have run in three Olympics and met some of the greatest coaches in the world. Babar Sahab is among the greatest of them. His training methods, motivation, and inspiration is fantastic.'*

In 1971 and 1972, Shri Ram Singh won gold and represented India in the Olympics. In 1974, Shri Ram Singh and Shivanth Singh won gold and silver at the Asian Games, and Shri Ram Singh also won gold at the international athletic meet. *'Jo aap karayenge, wo hum karenge'* (whatever you instruct us to do, we will absolutely do the same) was the attitude of all his athletes. The legendary coach used to say, *'My training is hard, which is why none of my boys has failed'*with obvious confidence.

Some people used to say that my grandpa was a 'psychotic' and Sri Ram Singh was a 'piece of piss,'a walk-over of outdated and wrong training. But he never responded to these allegations; instead, he let his work speak for itself. Even his basic right to wear religious clothing during training, disagreeing with long coaching camps, and employing his own coaching tricks and tactics were viewed as insurrectionary at times. At one marathon competition, a disciple of grandpa participated in a 20 km run. In such competitions, runners are timely supplemented with beverages for staying hydrated. Grandpa's pupil felt nauseous and started vomiting after drinking that. Grandpa caught the vomit right away in his hand & gave it to the forensic lab for testing. Some hazardous drug was detected, which was surely mixed in his drink during the game. Grandpa observed. Grandpa was sure that someone tried to let down his training skills out of envy. But he always ignored such tactics of people as *'Actions speak louder than words.'*

A situation came into Grandpa's life when he was seen through the eyes of suspicion due to his appearance and religion. I don't remember the exact year, but at that time there were some competitions going on abroad and grandpa's trainees also participated. Grandpa was curious to know the result. At 3 am, he went into the headquarters to check the result. People peeped at him going to the headquarters in the middle of the night suspiciously. He knew the results secretly and went back home. The next morning, word spread that a man from Pakistan had entered the headquarters the night before. When grandpa learned about the rumours, he inquired about the time. He realised it was a misunderstanding. 'Lieutenant Sir, I went to the headquarters to check the results,' he explained to everyone. Such situations can come to anyone's life, but the key here is to remain calm & confident. Though grandpa got into such situations in his life, he never hides his identity and gives up his faith out of fear. He always openly confessed his religion by wearing his white Kurta Pyjamas, keeping a long beard, and offering prayer wherever he liked; portraying a perfect prophetic look. He spent his entire life surrounded by a variety of people, including Rajputs, Hindus, Christians, Sikhs, Punjabis, lower caste, and upper caste, but never hesitated to have friendship with them. No matter what, he used to develop companionship irrespective of community and caste openly.

Soar to Heaven, Yet Keep Roots in the Earth

Undoubtedly, my grandfather was always hardworking, honest, and enthusiastic about his work. But when it came to competitions and championships, he would always tighten his belt to make sure he could run the extra mile for the sake of his country's name. Now it was time for the toughest practice for the upcoming 1976 Olympic Games in Montreal, Canada. The coach began with cross-country running and road races in Delhi. In the morning, he used to take them on a cross-country run of 8 to 10 km, and they used to spend the evening on the grass. Frequently, he used to train them on the lawns near India Gate, even in the dark. The practice regime was followed by two months of sand running in Okhla. He used to make them run for one and a half hours. Sometimes on the plains, sometimes on the hills. He used different methods to train the participants or competitors. They also used to play handball. In the six working days of the week, there would be two sessions a day, sometimes even three. Normally, they used to spend 5–6 hours in training.

In May and June, they began track and field work. Shri Ram Singh was allowed to compete in two events in Chandigarh, the 800 and 1500 meters. He won both at Chandigarh, clocking a new record of 13:45:6 in the 1500 m. It was now time for trials in Patiala, just a step close to Montreal. He again clocked a cool 1:47:3 in the trials. The poor coach pleaded a lot to send Shri Ram to Europe before straightaway sending him to Montreal, but no one listened to him. After that, there was a pre-Olympic meet in which athletes were divided and grouped into separate heats based on their pre-Game timings. Everybody left for Montreal, leaving my grandpa behind, who was needed there the most. Just five days before Shri Ram was to run his first heat, my grandpa expressed his desire to go to Montreal with no money and no passport in his hand. His friend helped him get his passport before lunch, and the same evening, he left for Montreal with one change and one hundred leaves of *paan* as his only luggage. But the rumours spread that after selling his house, utensils, and scooter, Babar managed to reach Montreal to watch his favourite athlete, Shri Ram.

It was unusual that some officials, who used to ignore Grandpa in Delhi, requested that he guide Shri Ram and said, 'Mulk ki izzat ab aapke haathoun mein hai' (The honor of the country is now in your hands). In the Olympic 800-meter program, the first heat was held on July 23rd. The following day was the semifinal, where Shri Ram Singh finished fourth. He was very tired after that, and his whole body was aching. His teammates helped him anyway. The next morning, Grandpa reached the gym and met everyone during the warm-up session. He shocked everyone. *'Run your own race; don't hold anything back; do not be nervous, you are bound to get a medal,'* said the master motivator to his star pupil. The bell rang, and the race began. My grandpa calmly sat in the stands, chewing his all-time favourite mouth freshener, *paan*. Shri Ram Singh crossed the finish line in 1:45:77, setting a new Olympic record. The other competitors and their clocking times were:

1. **Alberto Juantorena- Cuba**

Clocking time - 1:43:50 (world record)

2. **Ivo van Damme- Belgium**

Clocking time - 1:43:86

3. **Richard Wolhunter- America**

Clocking time - 1:44:12

4. **Willi Welbeck- Germany**

Clocking time - 1:45:44

5. **Steve Ovett- Britain**

Clocking time - 1:45:44

6. **Lucaiano Susany- Yugoslavia**

Clocking time - 1:45:75

7. **Shri Ram Singh Shekhawat- India**

Clocking time - 1:45:77

8. **Lastly, Carlo Crippo- Italy**

Clocking time - 1:48:39

As soon as the competition was over, the gold medalist, Alberto Juantorena, commented, 'I broke the record because of Singh.' He realised it, as Shri Ram Singh had the fastest basic speed among the top 800 -meter runners. Everybody was delighted at Shri Ram's record-breaking race except the disheartened coach. In a very low voice, he uttered, 'Shri Ram should have won the medal.' He thought a few elementary races would have made the difference between a medal and seventh place. But his voice was not heard, and he was overlooked.

Grandpa didn't compete above the national level as an athlete, but he always tried to present himself well to his pupils. He used to say that during competitions, while he used to sit in the stands and watch the ravishing waves of his athletes, he would feel as if he were on the track. Anyway, in Montreal, after spending his days on the field and nights in the mosque for two days, he was back home. When Shri Ram reached India, he was warmly welcomed, but the coach was sidelined as always! Shri Ram Singh clocked 1:45:77 and left behind the new Munich Olympic record, which stood for 40 years.

There was a mutual college friend of grandpa called Mr Khalid Zahidullah. In Osmania University, grandpa was addicted to athletics while his friend Mr Khalid sahab used to be a phenomenal basketball player at the national level. Later Mr Khalid sahab settled in the U.S. He used to always invite grandpa to visit the U.S. and get settled for the bright future of his children. When grandpa was in Montreal Mr Khalid sahab was desperately calling grandpa. He planned to call grandpa as soon as the completion is over in Montreal and insisted that grandpa should stay there till he finishes the legal work of the visa. Today, people spend many lakhs to travel the United States of America, but grandpa got lucky to visit the U.S. without spending a penny at that time. Still, he refused to take this chance due to his patriotism. He used to say, *'I will stay in India and work hard on Indians to get a name.'* Grandpa's exultation was that he always succeeded despite being surrounded by politics. He worked immensely hard to see the tricolour *'tirangaa'* fly high in international sports. Grandpa's dear friend Mr

P.K Mahanand sahab, used to always say, ‘Khan sahab; these people will never realise and pay back your services, so put a habit of speaking a bit.’ But the coach used to turn a deaf ear to him. He never thought to reach from rags to riches in his life, probably that was the reason behind his peace of mind & satisfaction with little money.

The following year, he represented Asia in the World Cup of Athletics. In 1978, the Asian Games were supposed to be held in Bangkok. Again, all his pupils flew to Bangkok, leaving the coach behind! He, too, wanted to go. Granny, on the other hand, did not let her husband go on his own expenses this time. She reasoned that if the sports agency authority could send all unimportant people abroad, why not the coach, who would be most needed by his trainees? In Bangkok, Shri Ram Singh, Geeta Zutshi, and Ratan Singh all performed well. A jury of coaches decided to choose Shri Ram Singh as "Asia’s Best Athlete," and he was given the "Adidas Golden Shoe Award." But there was a legend for which all experts eyes were looking. They announced him as "Asia’s Best Athletic Coach" and wanted to honour him with the "Adidas Golden Shoe Award," but alas! He was not there. The Golden Shoe Award was sent through the manager of the Indian athletic team to the well-deserving Indian athletic coach, also the only in Asia, Mohammed Ilyas Babar. He was the first Indian to receive this honour.

One day, Grandpa was travelling. On his route from Delhi to Hyderabad, his health began to deteriorate. He was forced to disembark from a moving train on the Agra platform.

Coincidentally, the ticket collector saw him getting off. He recognised him because he used to see Grandpa on trains most of the time. Grandpa started talking a lot and repeating his words, which was unlike his behaviour. The ticket collector caught hold of him and didn't let him go alone. He called the army centre and requested to dispatch Shri Ram Singh and inform them of Grandpa's condition. Shri Ram Singh arrived in Agra with other soldiers.

He spoke to somebody, and my grandpa was successfully taken to Hyderabad with a throng of people. He was diagnosed with a blood clot in the brain that made him react insensibly. His memory of the past twenty-two days was deleted. Dr Majid Khan, who was a good friend of grandpa, treated him for six months. After completing his treatment, grandpa shifted to Jamshedpur to join TISCO (Tata iron and steel company), as they were offering him work for so many days.

A Voice of Truth Awakens the Sleeping World

Jamshedpur, also known as "Tatanagar," was founded by Jamsetji Tata as a "steel city." It is in the Indian state of Jharkhand and the 15th - cleanest city in India. Jamshedpur is the reputed sports capital of Jharkhand, promoted by Tata Steel. The Tata group also owns the beautiful and large JDK sports complex stadium, which is used for a variety of sports activities. My grandpa moved to Jamshedpur in 1982 and started his work.

Although *tabligh* (a mission to enlighten people with Islamic knowledge) was always in his life, here it was at its height. He found doing *tabligh* more important in Jamshedpur because of the state of the Muslims living there. So much blood was spilt in the riots that took place before he moved here. The *fasadaat* (communal riots) developed a huge fear in Muslims, and it made them weak in their judgment. Muslim women used to wear *sindoor* (red vermillion powder) and *bindiya* (forehead dot) and walk uncovered in public to disguise themselves as non-Muslims. As a result, he took it as his highest responsibility, and in collaboration with his family and other noble men and women, he started *tabligh* with the goal to bring a positive change to society and assist Muslims in practising Islam.

B.D. Sharma was one of grandpa's trainees. He later moved to TELCO. He was so influenced by and fond of Grandpa that he used to keep Grandpa's photo along with the idols he worshipped. In TELCO, a coach was there who used to enjoy the company of my grandpa. He was a Hindu, and he was married to a Pundit. Grandpa used to spend quality time with him. The good conduct and unconditional love of Grandpa made that man accept Islam. He even acquired Islamic knowledge under the guidance of my grandfather.

Grandpa used to spend his weekends doing *tabligh*. Also, once every fifteen days, he used to spend time in the *jamaat* (communal congregation for faith renewal). My grandmother had a daily ritual of selecting a house to gather and counsel women on Islamic knowledge. On Sundays, she used to hold such counselling sessions at her house. She believed in the maxim that when a drop of water drips on a slimy stone every day, one day its smoothness and lubrication will not last. It will make it rough. Likewise, due to daily counselling and congregations, almost all the women gradually gave up doing non-Islamic acts and developed faith in God. Girls started to veil themselves. But in some colleges, it was not allowed. So, some *tablighi jammat* members decided to go with the college girls who wanted to veil. Nobody argued about the hijab; rather, it gave strength and courage to the other girls.

When talking about grandpa's *tabligh* work in Hyderabad, I can't forget grandpa's close friend Mr Tejvan Palle. He was also a sportsman and belonged to the Pillai caste. He used to stay in Secunderabad. After finishing his work, grandpa used to visit Mr Tejvan Palle sahab while returning home. Mr Tejvan sahab's father highly admired grandpa. He used to give great protocol to grandpa whenever he visited. He used to lay a prayer mat for grandpa and arrange water for doing ablution.

Mr Tejva's father used to memorise many surahs from my grandpa with great interest. He was very much influenced by Islam due to my grandpa's righteous company. When Mr Tejvan's father's health began to deteriorate, grandpa used to visit him frequently. He requested that after his death, his funeral bath should be given by grandpa. Also, his dead body should be buried rather than being taken to the pyre for cremation. Eventually, after his death, grandpa followed the funeral procession to the graveyard. Likewise, grandpa's company was enough to complete the faith of the people.

In Jamshedpur, his trainees Charles Borromeo won gold, and Geeta Zutshi won silver in the 110 meters. Everything was going well until the day he was called for a meeting. While conversing about things related to training, he noted an inadequacy in athletes' official money for sports expenditures and in the accounts of people sitting there. Right then, he began to write his resignation and waited in the wings for the meeting to wind up. Before he left, he submitted his resignation and, after reaching home, didn't let anyone know. When Granny came to know from outsiders that her husband had left the job, she was very disappointed. 'Something you're supposed to inform me of, I've heard from others,' Granny said sadly. 'Mumtaz, nothing special; if I had told you at once, then again you would have started giving me lectures like the home minister. As you know, I can't bear unfairness with my boys, and here, everyone is filling their pockets. They offered me as well. And what is there in losing a job? Today I lost; tomorrow I will find another,' added the coach convincingly.

Grandpa never had job satisfaction at TISCO. Eventually, he packed up to return to Delhi with the spirit of soon producing a string of middle and long-distance runners and dominating the scene in India. In his absence during the Seoul Asian Games of 1986, not a single male athlete from India won a gold medal in the track events. A full day of *ishtema* (a gathering of Islamic counselling) was held to bid farewell to my grandpa and his family as they were actively involved in *tabligh*.

In Humility Before Humanity, in Devotion Before the Divine

Grandpa soon returned to the army to experience the discipline of the army and the systematic life of an army center. They lived in a spacious, nice house with a good kitchen garden. Granny used to plant saplings and sow seeds of vegetables in her garden. It was a very clean area. Peacock sounds could be heard, and sometimes they used to fly to their garden as well. There were also some henna trees around. Women would pluck the henna leaves, rub them on stones, and then apply them to their hands. The neighbourhood consisted of Rajastanis and Punjabis, but there were no Muslims. Granny also used to sow garlic and onions; inspired by the Rajastanis, she used to harvest tons of onions and garlic.

When Grandpa resumed his work, he elevated the current Indian athletics scheme. He proposed to choose teens of 12 to 13-year-olds and train them for the 1992 Olympics or the 1988 Seoul Games. He also recommended that athletes obtain constant training: nine months at home and three months abroad. He also added that international exposure would help athletes more than coaching and trending equipment. Furthermore, he stated that sportspeople should be given good jobs so that young people and juniors are encouraged to participate in sports. When his athletes struggled to win a medal, he used to feel that they were not being given adequate competition. He trusted the Western pattern of practice. To upgrade the standards, India has only three levels: state, international, and open. He was sure that his trainee had the desire to improve.

The group of new runners would commence their day at 5 o'clock by running on sand. From RRRC, they would jog down to the nearby Narain Pahari. They would then start running up the steep slope twenty-five times before jogging back down the hill. After breakfast, they would sprint up the slope for sixty minutes. The early morning routine was followed by a second segment at 10 a.m. for supervision. My grandpa used to give individual attention to each runner, weed out their defects, help them with weightlifting exercises, and sort their routines. He firmly believed that every athlete is a separate individual who has different motivational levels and should use different methods of training. From 3:30 to 5:30 or 6 p.m., he used to take his boys to the tracks. He was one of the few coaches who had a knack for motivating athletes by understanding their psychology and toughening them mentally. He observed that even the mind plays a crucial part. He used to say, *"Unless an athlete is brave and mentally tough, how can he win in a big contest?"* At one national, Shri Ram Singh was hesitant, but Grandpa encouraged him that he could beat his rivals with yards to spare. His pupils had confidence in his clean life, hard work, and the sincerity of his intentions. Perhaps that's why they were able to confront the best Asian athletes with courage.

Dina Ram was one of Grandpa's students. He was a low-profile army man. Nobody believed that this man could make India proud. But when he won the 300-meter steeplechase gold medal barefoot and took the silver medal at the Beijing Games in 1989, he left everybody speechless. Now, when he won both gold and silver, grandpa was confident that Dina Ram could do India proud by making it to the finals of the Tokyo Championship and possibly winning a medal in the Barcelona Olympics of 1999. He also added that it would be possible if Dina Ram were allowed to gain international experience. His star student, Shri Ram Singh, too, began coaching. He began to receive good offers as he acquired brilliant training skills from my grandpa. Soon after, he was hired by the government to work in the army.

Grandpa never adorned himself with a garment that cost an arm and a leg. Whether it was an award ceremony or if he was invited as a chief guest, he used to only wear old, clean clothes that were properly ironed, a skull cap, a stone finger ring, and a watch as his accessories. He was once invited to be the guest of honour at the Institute of Athletics, West Bengal's fourth sports day celebration. It was held in 1979 at Eden Gardens in Kolkata. Despite carrying an extra, newly stitched pair of kurta pyjamas, he attended the ceremony in the same clothes he had worn throughout his travels. When he was backing home, Granny showed her disappointment in Grandpa's unsophisticated habits. 'Mumtaz, clothes are not everything. Everyone was happy with my presence alone, as they thought I wouldn't come because of the media and my preeminence.' He eschewed both popularity and advertency, which are significant features in the Indian sporting outlook. He never wore a blazer, never hankered after shows, and never gave any press interviews. Nonetheless, he used to capture people's attention and praise.

At times when granny used to be in Hyderabad, grandpa would visit Hyderabad to spend time with his family. The news of my grandpa's arrival in Hyderabad used to spread like wildfire. Grandma would ask what to make for lunch regularly. Once, when granny asked him, he very longingly told her, 'I want to eat Biryani.' 'Why do you want Biryani at the wrong time? If you're that hungry, I'll make Dalcha and Baghara Khaana instead,' Granny quickly added. Grandpa, on the other hand, was adamant about having Biryani. No matter how much he forced her, Granny didn't listen and didn't ask anyone to bring the groceries. Simultaneously, grandpa cried, 'It is absolutely fine if there is no lunch; I will eat only biryani today and nothing else.' He had a strong heartfelt wish and was sure that God would feed him Biryani that day. Later, they heard an automobile parking in front of the house. When Granny saw him, it was her uncle who came to see Grandpa after hearing about his presence in Hyderabad. 'I have come to meet Babar Bhai; I am going to Shahabad from here,' the man informed her, unloading the food from the auto rickshaw. 'What is in the dish?' Granny inquired. 'Tameez (uncle's daughter) has sent delicious goat meat Biryani, dabal ka meetha (sweet bread), and some special items from our bakery,' uncle answered. Granny was amazed to see the Biryani. It is truly said and proven that if one has complete trust in God and seeks everything only from him, then God will surely reward his servant according to his faith and intentions.

Embrace Triumph and Let Envy Fade into Silence

The Indian athletic community very soon realized the contributions of my grandpa to Indian sports. It is truly said that "*There is a right time for everything to happen in life.*" After working for more than three decades in military games, the Dronacharya award emerged as a reward in 1994. The Dronacharya Award is given to outstanding coaches in sports and games. It is the sports coaching honour of the Republic of India. It is awarded every year by the Ministry of Youth Affairs and Sports to the recipients who have done outstanding and meritorious work on a constituent basis and enabled sportspersons to excel in international events.

My Grandpa learnt about it through a friend and a younger coach, P.V. Ravannam, who heard it on the radio. He approached grandpa with some sweets and apprised him about the greatest forthcoming achievement of his life. Surprisingly, for more than a week, he didn't receive any official proclamation; nonetheless, it appeared in the newspaper. At the time when it was officially confirmed, my grandpa was having dinner. Grandpa received kudos from every person who heard of the Dronacharya victory. All his pupils were gathered in front of his house and were elated. But the poker-faced grandpa was patient. He used to balance his emotions by neither worrying too much in tough times nor crossing his limits in joy.

Before the award ceremony was held, all the recipients were given instructions on how and when to enter and where the president would be. Everything was communicated ahead of time to avoid inconvenience. The whole family was invited to the ceremony, but only his sons and his friends attended. Along with Grandpa, Sachin Tendulkar, another notable figure, shared a platform with him. When it was Ilyas Babar's turn, people gave him a big round of applause. In the audience, Shri Ram Singh was joyfully cheering. Grandpa's head had always bowed only before God in the prayer. Even the president was moved when he walked up the dais. As always, my God-fearing Grandpa was grateful to his Lord. 'I hope to work better in the future,'he humbly commented.

The award currently consists of a bronze statuette of Dronacharya, a certificate, a ceremonial gown, and a cash prize of 15 lakh rupees. But way back in 1994, my grandpa received a statuette, a scroll, and a cash prize of seventy thousand rupees. My grandfather is the 11th sports celebrity to receive the prestigious Dronacharya award for coaching athletes to the highest level of athletic performance. Grandpa was satisfied to receive the award, but he regretted wearing the official blazer given by the sports authority in spite of his religious clothes. After receiving the award, he said it was a gratifying surprise for him. He also mentioned, 'How does the country or Indian athletics benefit from it? It would have been better to make use of my services rather than give awards at the tail end of my career. It's all God's grace; *der aae durust aae* (better late than never!)'

To get to the sports ground, grandpa used to travel by bicycle. As a result, his legs and body would swell up. He did not receive a golden handshake despite winning the Dronacharya award. Granny suggested, 'If they neither enhance the salary nor give any other provisions, then you should resign.' He was incapable of buying a house and always encircled himself within the limits of his need. He was thrilled to bits with what God had offered him. Even though he had a huge family, he never asked for any facilities. I recollect, When the media arrived to report on Grandpa's death, they were astounded to see where he lived. He lived in an average house with no car parked in front of his gate; there was neither a sofa set in the house nor any other household essentials. However, he habitually lived this pattern of life throughout his life span and was the happiest and most satisfied man I have ever known. When they were just debating about his current job, Grandpa was promptly invited by the Amateur Athletic Association of West Bengal (AAAWB, 1995) to train the thirteen Bengal senior athletes who were selected for the ensuing SAF games. So, he left for Kolkata to discuss and have a glance at the work. But he didn't quit the RRRC yet.

My grandpa's success made people happy and envious as well. Grandpa had a neighbour who was always keeping an eye on visitors to his house and wanted to know where he was. His suspicions prompted him to inquire from Granny. But Grandma totally denied answering any question of him, saying that he should have no concern about it. Two days later, a picture of Grandpa with athletes on the field got printed in the newspaper. After hearing the rumours and nursing false assumptions, a letter was sent to Granny, formerly, to shift from the cantonment area in grandpa's absence.

Unlike her husband, Granny was of quite the opposite nature. She confidently went to the commander and said that he had no right to send her this letter. She told him to give this letter to those who work for him in the military. 'If I implement your notice, stand outside the house with my children and belongings, and call the media, complaining about your behaviour with a Dronacharya-awarded family, then you will be nowhere,' she added. The commander then apologised to Granny and cleared up the misunderstanding that he had.

Grandpa submitted his resignation immediately after he reached Hyderabad. He terminated the journey with RRRC with an aching heart and packed up to move to Hyderabad. Almost the entire crowd came out of the centre to see them off with tears as they walked out. Ladies were saying, *'Phir aana maim sab, behenji, phiraana.'* (Come again). It was the end of his most favourite life—the life of discipline, the life of Delhi.

Roaring Success Blossoms from Devotion and Dedication

Moving to Hyderabad, grandpa settled in Red hills. He was a native of Red hills since he was four years old. People knew him as a peacemaker of the Red Hills. Aged people used to call him grandpa, and Babar Bhai was on the tongue of children. During riots, when there used to be curfews, all the houses used to be deserted except the terrace of grandpa's house. While patrolling, police used to stop by Grandpa's house, wait a while and leave without saying a word. While the backstreet of his house was accommodated by Hindus, the other road was covered with a couple of houses owned by Christians. During the kite festival, there used to be disputes among the kite flyers. Everybody would run towards Grandpa to get justice. After listening to both parties, Grandpa would scold someone, punish someone and then he would ask to bring sweets and celebrate the festival together. When there used to be 'Eid ul Fitr, his pupils used to say, '*guruji ke yahan kal Eid hai, kuch mat banaiyo, bahut khana milega kal wahaan.*' (Tomorrow it is Eid; don't cook anything; a lot of food will be offered to us.) And they used to enjoy *mash ke wade, namak pare,* and *sheer khurma,* made by granny, throughout the night. On Holi and Diwali, all his pupils and their wives would visit Grandpa with a lot of sweets to celebrate. My grandmother's kitchen would be full of kilos of sweets. They used to put a *tilak* on granny's forehead and a *rang* on grandpa's hand, touch their feet, and take their blessings. As I described, people from different regions and religions used to have this kind of understanding.

There was not a single dispute in the whole life of Grandpa related to social status, caste and religion. Rather, it was one huge family whose network was well-maintained with love and concern by Grandpa. He never let anyone poison the heart with communal differences and rivalries.

Grandpa shortly signed an agreement with the sports authority of India for two years and left for Bangalore. Here he was responsible for training non-army men. At the beginning, he was staying alone, but later, one of his family members would join him, making it a vacation hub. Grandpa was once accompanied by my parents and my youngest uncle. On one afternoon, grandpa was mellowing at home. My uncle hesitatingly switched on the television. While he was randomly changing the channels, grandpa cried, 'Stop! Let's watch this movie.' It was an American western film, Mackenna's Gold, which they watched that afternoon. Grandpa was fond of watching movies and clicking pictures in his youth. But later, when he came to know it was a sin, he gave up everything. Here in Bangalore grandpa apart from his work, also used to spend most of his time with his family.

Returning to Hyderabad after two years, nobody knew that his honour was incomplete till the chief minister of his own state venerated him with the Telugu Aatma Gaurava Dinatsavam award. He was presented with this award in 1999. Mr N. Chandrababu Naidu, who was the CM of Andhra Pradesh, handed over a cash prize of fifty thousand rupees and asked him to render his services in the Gachibowli stadium, Hyderabad, as a professional athletic coach As a result, Grandpa accepted his offer and joined. Notwithstanding his employment as a coach at Gachibowli Stadium, he never stopped applying to the Sports Authority of India (SAI) and military services. He showed his willingness to the vice chairman and MD of SAI, AP, to let him train state athletes for both the national games and the Pusan Asian Games of 2002. He worked like a charm and proved himself for more than four decades. He was simultaneously exploring all avenues to get back into military sports service. Grandpa presented his desire to coach the army athletes, first for the 2002 Asian Games in Pusan and then for the 2004 Olympic Games in Athens. He wrote letters as well as visited Delhi many times, showing his enthusiasm. But none came forward to support him in his venture.

In the year 1966, under grandpa's training, an athlete called Arjun Bhogeswar Barua won gold in the international event. On the birthday of Arjun Bhogeswar Barua (B.S. Barua) every year, Abhiruchi Sports Day is organised by the state of Assam to mark the life of B.S. Barua as a living sporting legend. On September 3, 2001, the 35th Abhiruchi Sports Day was held in Guwahati, and Grandpa was invited as the chief guest. B.S. Barua was delighted to have my grandpa on his promising day.

My grandpa's career was regular but distinguished, simple yet inspiring, and came up with themes like *'do the job you love, rather than love the job you do.'* His career serves as the best example of one's love for and satisfaction with one's work. He soulfully felt worthy of himself when he made his country proud in international sports. The former was the sole aim of grandpa, which he achieved at the end of his career. He was always ahead of his time in his teaching skills. Perhaps he never used to jot down his pre-training schedule, which was spontaneous and perfect for his profession. Grandpa was joyful despite his deteriorating health and financial pressure. Even in his final days, he expressed a strong desire to be appointed to train athletes for the upcoming Pusan and Athens games. But none came forward. Eventually, the remarkable career of Mohammed Ilyas Babar reached the finish line. The zealous, the first proud Indian to receive the prestigious Adidas Golden Shoe award, hoped to produce more gold medalists, but it sadly ended as his last wish.

Babar sahab; once a Khiladi, always a coach

(a)

(b)

(c)

(d)

(a), (b), (c), (d) Babar sahab furnished star pupil Shri Ram Singh and transformed him from an athlete to a skilful coach

(a)

(b)

(a) & (b) Babar sahab with the Bengal youth on the inauguration ceremony of AAAWB's SAF special game camp at the SAI complex in the Salt Lake

Babar sahab with P.T Usha

Babar sahab with Dina Ram

Bihar state meet Bokaro 1984

Young Babar sahab (middle) with his pupils Nausha, Saroja and others

Babar sahab with trainee Shri Ram Singh (middle) and friend Mr P.K Mahanand (left)

Babar sahab with pupil Tarlok Singh

Babar sahab with the commander of the Rajputana Rifles Regimental Centre on the occasion of Eid-ul-fitr

Babar sahab of 50s

(a)

(b)

(c)

(a), (b), (c) - Babar sahab with sports officials & other men multiplying smiles on Eid-ul-fitr

Babar sahab's joyful moments with Flying Singh

Babar sahab with prestigious Dronacharya award

Babar sahab with son Mohammed Haseeb Babar (extreme left) & friend Mr P.K Mahanand (extreme right) outside Rashtrapati Bhavan, New Delhi

Babar sahab receiving the Dronacharya award by the former president of India Mr Shankar Dayal Sharma (1995)

(a)

(b)

(c)

(a), (b), (c) - Babar sahab invited as a chief guest at the 35th Abhiruchi sports day, Guwahati

(a)

(b)

(c)

(a), (b), (c) - A mass rally event held on Abhiruchi sports day to give notability to Babar sahab

(a)

(b)

(c)

(a), (b), (c) - Babar sahab and his pupil B.S Barua

Babar sahab with B.S Barua and his family

Joyful memories with Shri Ram Singh

Telugu Aatma Gaurava Dinatsavam award given to Babar sahab by the govt. of A.P, 1999

Babar sahab with chief minister of A. P Mr.Chandrababu Naidu and other officials

Ilyas Babar gymnasium (above)
A memorial built by the respected Indian army, a tribute given to Babar sahab

Ilyas Babar Gymnasium: a homage (established in 2007, situated in New Delhi, Army Centre)

Simplicity is the Spring of Blessings

Grandpa had his own way of extracting money from granny. 'I have seen such a beautiful doll in the shop for you.' He would say, and launder money from her. After getting the money, he used to annoy Granny a lot; he would make excuses that the shop was closed, etc., and neither return the money nor bring anything. After a couple of days, when Granny's anger would cool a bit, he would again trick her, saying, 'Oh wow! What a doll I saw today in the shop,' and Granny would melt again.

There was nothing like the first meeting in the case of my grandparents. As they were first cousins, they used to live in a common house and had the same upbringing. With these innocent and cherishable memories, grandpa grew into a skilled and decent man, and granny bloomed into a beautiful young lass. Granny used to love attending the wedding rituals during the *Shaadi* season. When she heard that many people were offering marriage proposals to Grandpa, she was excited and anticipated the commencement of marriage functions for her childhood cousin. But the Almighty God is the best of planners. Only he knows what benefits us more than ourselves. Let me break the monotony of the word "my grandpa" here and narrate the rest of the story to you by addressing my grandfather as "Babar sahab."

In the year 1958, when Babar sahab was leaving for Khadakwasla, the grandfather of Babar sahab proposed that 'if there is a girl present in our house, then what is the need to look outside?' He suggested that their parents think about it and ask their children whether they want each other or not. My grandparents showed allegiance and agreed to abide by the elders' decision. At the eleventh hour, Babar sahab got engaged to his cousin Mumtaz, with whom he used to quarrel a lot. But he also had a soft corner. Perhaps the elders' decision was not a bolt from the blue for him!

In a few months, while Babar sahab was working in Fatehgarh, he instantly made up his mind to go back to Hyderabad, as people around him used to frequently offer marriage proposals. In the year 1960, the *nikaah* ceremony was held very simply, without any waste of money. Even the food was cooked at home without any expert chefs. A goat was cut, and the meal was prepared. Babar sahab was on leave for fifteen days, and immediately left after it was over. Within two months, Granny and her mother-in-law joined him. They followed him to Patiala to let him have his training.

Babar sahab's early life was quite regular. Granny was not an alien to Babar sahab as they grew up together. To develop further understanding as a couple, he used to take Granny to his official functions and hang out with her. He also used to take her to restaurants on his wedding anniversaries and would buy a gift for her rather than celebrating it and making it westernised. Once Babar sahab took Granny to explore the delicate Taj Mahal during the full moon. But on that day, it was closed for outsiders due to the arrival of Queen Elizabeth. Hence, they visited later. Though granny still says that her previous visit did not go in vain. She says as if she saw a *moum ki gudiya* (a doll made of wax) on earth.

Babar sahab married life was an ideal one. I would not exaggerate if I can describe him as an ideal husband. He was a one-woman man who sincerely kept his feelings to himself before getting married to Granny and confessed it after the wedding. But a relationship does not become successful only by being sincere with each other. Respect and security hold and retain each other's happiness like the root holds a tree. In this transient world, Babar sahab fulfilled all the needs of his wife. When it comes to respect, at times when Granny used to be a little angry with Babar sahab, he would politely say, 'Look at your mother's anger today.' No matter how much Granny rages on him, Babar sahab's mouth would be sealed. He always used to take advice from granny, saying that 'Mumtaz's advice is very satisfying.' Moving on to the family of his wife, he was like an elder brother to his sisters-in-laws and an inspiration to his brother-in-laws. All were under the security of Babar sahab till they got married. Granny says that as much as she defines & appreciates her husband is less. Whenever she goes to a wedding, she would pray the same to every bride, 'May God give a husband like me to every girl.' This statement alone is enough to narrate the versatility of Babar sahab as a life partner. His personality was further elevated when he carried his first child, Ayesha Sabina, in the year 1963.

Fulfil Your Duty and Let the Divine Hold the Rest

Many years ago, as my grandpa's parents went through a divorce, his mother never let her son learn about his father. Who is he? What is his identity? These are natural questions that arise in the mind of a child when he observes other fathers and attempts to inquire about his missing parent. Although Babar sahab grew up young, got married, and became a father himself, he never stopped asking questions about his father. Obviously, his mother was silent, but others answered his questions. It helped him find his father after so many years, but in an unhealthy state. He used to look after him, make sure he had his meals properly each day, buy him new clothes, and take care of everything that was needed. When his mother came to know about his covert meetings with his father, she asked, 'Why do you meet and take care of him when he never tried to find out about you and never spent a penny on you?' My righteous Babar sahab replied, 'The relationship between you and him no longer exists, but I am his son; I have to fulfil my duty, otherwise God will question me on the Day of Accountability. I will answer about my deeds, and he is supposed to answer about his.' These words satisfied his mother and calmed her anger.

Babar sahab rented a room in the mosque for his father's stay. He used to pay him daily visits while he was in Hyderabad and keep an eye on him. But when he was in Delhi, his father used to wander wherever he liked. One day, when Babar sahab was in Hyderabad due to his work, he saw his father in a bad condition. He decided to take his father to Delhi and has begun to prepare.

In Delhi, his mother visited to spend her holidays with her son and daughter-in-law. She was eagerly waiting to see her son and kiss his forehead lovingly when he returned. But she became suspicious when she dreamt that a pious, white-bearded man was telling her, 'Your son is going to find his father and come to you along with him.' The following day, as soon as she saw her ex-husband and son stepping out of the jeep and entering through the gate, she straightaway went inside and packed her luggage. Despite Babar sahab's firm insistence, she did not relent and left for Hyderabad the same evening.

Babar sahab's father was addicted to alcohol. Now that he was living with his son, who was a true practitioner of Islamic dos and don'ts, he was kept away from it. As he was suddenly prohibited from drinking alcohol without any treatment, his health started to decline rapidly. Although the doctor advised Babar sahab to give him liquor occasionally in small quantities, But Babar sahab refused. Eventually, the aged man was prescribed complete bed rest by his doctor. Babar sahab chose to see his father as a sick man rather than as a drunkard before God on the day of the Resurrection.

Granny suggested to her husband that he admit her father-in-law to a hospital as she was expecting her fourth child, and it was not manageable for her to look after a patient properly. But Babar sahab declined her idea and decided to take care of his father himself. Daily, after reaching home from his work, he would first do his father's work. After changing his tracksuit, he would first clean his father, as he was not in the condition to even walk to the washroom. Then he would give him a "lifebuoy bath" and even wash his dirty clothes.

Although he never used to do even his own work—he never even washed a hanky—he did everything for the service of his father, which pleases God. Babar sahab used to not feel like having a meal after cleaning his father and other stuff, so granny used to make morsels and put them in his mouth. When Granny used to feel sorry for her husband, he would say, ‘No, Mumtaz, he is my father. Who is responsible for looking after him if I don't?’

During the last days of his father, when the barber used to come to shave his beard, the old man used to refuse. Babar sahab used to be pleased when he saw his father's righteousness, because it meant that his father had finally found the right path and was carrying out Islamic law. Just before his death, he called Granny, gave her his blessings, and said, ‘If you give birth to a baby boy, name him Ahmed, as that is my name.’ Every person indeed dies for their deeds. But it is also true that the intentions of the deeds, the purity of the heart, and the respect for religion are things only God knows well.

The father of Babar sahab remembered God and his messenger in his last breaths and died reading the *shahadah* (the testimony of the oneness of God and belief in the last prophet). The funeral was carried honourably by Muslim recruits, kernels, generals, majors, and other friends of Babar sahab. At last, Babar sahab was peaceful as his father died the way he wanted him to die with dignity, forgiveness, and remembrance of Almighty God. In a couple of years, Babar sahab's mother also passed away when she got settled in Delhi after her retirement.

Fatherhood is the Covenant of Peace, Sacrifice and Kinship

Babar sahab's life was not less than that of a nomad.

In the year 1967, when Babar sahab joined his beloved military service, he used to be away from home for longer spells. When he used to visit Hyderabad, he would stay with his family at a house which was both his and granny's inheritance. Later on, when it was sold, they moved to Rethibowli and finally to rented houses. Granny was always satisfied to live in Hyderabad. After the death of his parents, Babar sahab continued to live in Delhi for many years. By the passage of time, his loneliness was filled with the laughter of his growing children. He was blessed with five boys and four girls: Ayesha Sabina who was born in 1963, followed by; Mohammed Salahuddin Babar, Abdullah Babar, Ahmed Raza, Sara Fatima, Abdul Wasay, Khatija Saba, Safia Sana and lastly Mohammed Haseeb Babar born in 1984. Along with his vast family, Babar sahab was blessed with a wide circle of friends from his school, college, and his disciples. When he started *tabligh,* he was blessed with more devoted gentlemen. Mr Abdur Rehman Kazmi sahab is a veterinarian. He is the only friend of Grandpa who is alive. Mr Ikramuddin Wahaj sahab, who was an engineer. He passed even before the death of Babar sahab. Mr. pasha sahab, who spent his whole life fighting in courts. Every work of Babar sahab seemed to be incomplete without the involvement of Pasha sahab. As long as Babar sahab was hospitalised during his last days, Pasha sahab supported his family thoroughly. Although other friends used to formally visit him, Pasha sahab was staying like a full-time attender with Babarsahb's family. Now I mention Mr Kabir Ahmed sahab, who was a director in All - India Radio Station. Babar sahab first met him in Nizamuddin Markaz. At times, when Mr Kabir sahab would get a chance, he would sing a song on the radio, and just before that, he would call and alert Babar sahab. He was also one of those jewels who was by the side of Babar sahab in his last hours. The list continues with Mr Waheed sahab, who was in agriculture, Mr Mohammed Hamid sahab, Mr Azeem sahab, Mr Malik sahab, who owned a huge property and Mr. Basheeruddin sahab. Like granny says, they all portray the statues of real friends with distinguishing qualities. It is rightly said, *"The religion of a person depends on the religion of his company."* As religion was the priority of Babar sahab, he chose righteous people as his friends.

Despite having a huge family and even big responsibility of running the house alone, Babar sahab never took any favours. While living in the cantonment area, Babar sahab used to get a monthly pay of Rs. 3500/-. That little amount used to be enough for their food, shopping, and weekend outings, and if there used to be emergencies, Granny used to have money for those as well. For some children, they had to pay a fee, but for others, it was free because they were in army schools. As for the house rent and bills, they were not supposed to pay for either of them. Even the canteen was wholesale for them. That is why they used to manage such a small amount. But whenever Babar sahab used to be unemployed, they used to cut down on their meals, but would never ask for favours. I recollect there were two shagirds of Babar sahab in Delhi. One of them humbly brought a television, saying, 'You keep it.' His name was Devi. The other brought a refrigerator. He said, 'I need it, but I will take it when I go back to my village.' His name was Prasad. 'Look, I don't take other people's belongings,' Babar sahab clarified to him. 'You keep it for as long as you want, and then you take it away.' In one corner of the house, the refrigerator was kept, and on it, the TV was placed. 'Look, Devi and Prasad are sitting together,' family members would giggle. When Babar sahab was moving to Hyderabad, he instantly called them and asked them to take their belongings. Anyhow, both were forcing him to keep it. But Babar sahab, maintaining his self - respect said, 'No, no, we don't need anything. Come and take it, or else I'll put it outside.' Then both came and took their stuff. Even on insistence, he never used to take favours, no matter how much he had to suffer.

Babar sahab used to always appreciate Granny for her capabilities. It was very difficult for Granny to frequently travel with nine children and adjust to different places every time. Apart from taking care of the children, Granny was also fond of keeping pets at home from the very beginning. She used to raise chickens, rabbits, squirrels and even today she has many pairs of Australian birds caged in her sitting area. When her children began to grow they developed the same interest. Other than keeping dogs, monkeys, and owls, my father also dared to pet a snake and a scorpion with much interest. But Babar sahab was least bothered. He was only fond of painting when it comes to his hobby. He was also fond of eating and was a big foodie. He used to love desi and spicy food and would have anything offered to him without judging it, even if it was a dry leftover chapatti. He used to like eating *jowar roti* with *baingan ka bharta* or *muli ka thesa.* When someone from Gulbarga would arrive without *gurh phalli ki puri* (jaggery and peanut paratha), he would be surprised and ask, 'How come you came from Gulbarga and didn't bring gurh phalli ki puri?' He would love to eat chilli pickle oil with steamed cooked rice served hot. He was a crazy tea lover and used to drink 2-3 cups of tea in one sitting. During Ramadan, he would take advance salary and used to spend the whole month with his family and worshipping God. He used to observe all 30 fasts zestfully even at the age of 76. Also, during fasting, he used to say 'Wasn't it be nice if God had allowed to drink tea during fasts?' From the afternoon itself, he used to get worried and say 'look children, there won't be any iftar today, your mother has not gone into the kitchen yet.' Granny used to confidently reply, 'Will you be happy if I prepare everything and serve the best to you in time?' *Dahi vade* and boiled *chana* were the two staple dishes prepared by Granny throughout Ramadan.

Babar sahab never felt a burden to be the only bread earner of such a huge family. He lived his life to the fullest despite having nothing. He used to say, 'If there is peace within life, then man is healthy. What is there to worry about when you have left everything in God? God has promised to give; he will not let anyone sleep hungry. If today we sleep in hunger, tomorrow he will give. If not tomorrow, then the day after tomorrow, he will definitely give. God does not lack food to give.'

Despitc living with a low income, Babar sahab was not a stingy, typical man who asks for monthly expenditure from his wife. He used to happily hand over all his income to is wife. Even for buying new clothes, Granny used to shop for him. Four or five pairs of kurta pyjamas, one sweater, two sets of footwear and a bunch of skull caps used to easily serve the needs of Babar sahab for a year or more. But like most men, he was too fond of perfumes and used to buy them whatever it cost. Orange colored Jovan Musk was his favourite perfume, and even today, my father and uncle use that to smell like their father. That was all Babar sahab owned. His simple living was not a compromise to fulfil his family's needs but to achieve the pleasure of God.

I guess it was 1985 when Babar sahab moved to Jamshedpur and joined TISCO. With no job satisfaction, Babar sahab had to continue working in RRRC in Delhi. While living this nomadic life, Babar sahab's children completed their schooling in different schools of Hyderabad, Delhi and Jamshedpur. The responsibility to look after children's education always fell on granny. Babar sahab was a lenient father when it came to studies, as he himself never showed any interest in studies.

Babar sahab used to make sure everyone had a complete peace of mind and used to spend time with his children. He used to teach his daughters to ride a scooter despite being very religious. He never had any objection to his wife and daughters going on an outing. But he never allowed them to wear make-up. He used to appreciate his daughters when they cooked and gave money as a prize. Babar sahab used to take his sons to masjids and also spend time with them in *jamats* (congregation). He used to punctually gather his family members in the evening and enlighten them with the Prophet's sayings. Babar sahab was not prone to illness. If he ever used to fall sick, then he would say, 'Oh my, there is no one to enquire about my well-being.' He would then call his children one by one. All he wanted was for everyone to sit close to him. Randomly, he would ask everyone to stamp his legs, to quell his head, and so on. 'Your mother doesn't have time from her housekeeping chores to come and look after the patient lying here,' he would exaggeratedly tell Granny. In this way, he used to create humour and make sure no one destroys thc pleasant environment of his house. With such harmony, he brought up his children and settled in Hyderabad in the latter part of his life.

Babar sahab never forced any of his children to pursue their father's career. He only supported them in their interests. He was particular about two things. Firstly, he taught his children to never use his name to get any work done and to achieve everything on their own. Secondly, he taught them to earn from halal sources. Babar sahab wanted my father (Salah Uddin Babar) and Abdullah uncle to do hifz (memorisation of the Quran) so he admitted them into a *madarsa* (educational institution). Abdullah uncle also used to take cricket training from Mr Rahmat Baig during his schooling. He wanted to pursue cricket as his career, so Babar sahab agreed with it. Likewise, Haseeb uncle, who was the youngest of all, was another crazy sports spirit in Babar's house. He was also very ambitious to build a career in cricket. He used to go to the ground with his father during his schooling. Babar sahab used to train him for a marathon. Looking at the busy schedule of uncle, granny objected, 'From now itself you started training him for his game, he will definitely lag in his studies. Do one thing, now he is in school, so you don't give him any training until he graduates.' Hence, Babar sahab promised Haseeb uncle to resume his training after his graduation. When talking about girls, Babar sahab admitted them in private institutions to study till 10th standard as he didn't want them to study in co-ed. Once, the youngest girl of Babar sahab failed in the finals of intermediate. Babar sahab brought the sweets before the result was declared. When he learned that her daughter couldn't pass the examination, he did not react. He stayed impassive. He used to say that his children may not succeed in the eyes of the world, but for him, they were all winners. Like a carefree father, Babar sahab never pressured his children to hold positions and take degrees. Nor did he ever ask his sons to earn money even when he was 76 years old. All he asked his children was to offer the five-time prayer at the right time. That's all.

Babar sahab with Mr Salahuddin Babar (eldest son)

Mr Abdullah Babar (elder son)

Babar sahab with Abdul Wasay Babar (younger son)

Babar sahab with Mohammed Haseeb Babar (youngest son)

Babar sahab's middle son, Late. Ahmed Raza

Courage Amid the Trials of Life, Kindles Noble Action

Among his nine children, he had five boys. Out of five, three inherited the "sports gene" of their father. They were ambitious to built a career in sports like their father. Ahmed Raza *urf* 'Bablu' was the third son of Babar sahab. Like his brothers, he was also crazy about his game, cricket, since childhood. In 1993 or 1994, I don't remember the exact year, on one Friday, he was selected for the national team of Andhra Pradesh. Bablu uncle was twenty years old at that time. On the day he got selected, it had been only a few days when Babar sahab left for Delhi for work. Bablu uncle was on cloud nine and wanted to start the practice from the same evening. Even though Granny suggested taking a breath, he declined and left for the practice.

All the team members gathered on the ground, and it was a local friendly match when they began to play. While taking a catch, his fellow teammate called Shankar, and Uncle Raza didn't realise that they were confronting each other, as their eyes were fixed to the sky and on the ball. The teammate was shorter than Uncle Raza. Within seconds, the head of his teammate accidentally hit my uncle's chin so forcefully that my uncle fell back and got hurt by a stone on his head. There was no bleeding! He was taken straight to the hospital. My granny's brother reached the hospital earlier than the others. When Granny's brother finished talking with the doctor and went outside, he was shocked to see Uncle Raza lying on the stretcher, breathless!

Granny was panicky and went to the hospital, after which she went to the Sarojini Army Centre in Hyderabad to recount her son's tragedy. Granny asked the commander to make a call to immediately send Babar Sahab to Hyderabad. She asked him to make an excuse for his son's illness without disclosing the actual reason. Only family members and army people knew the truth at this point. They tried hard to conceal this from the media, but somehow it got leaked and was printed in the newspaper that *Babar suffered a blow on the same ground from where he got fame.* So on Sunday, the commander confiscated all the newspapers. In the meantime, he sent a word to call Babar sahab, saying 'Your wife called. Her name is Mumtaz, right? Your son is not well; he fell to the ground. Maybe she called out of anxiety,' the commander informed him. Babar sahab wondered, Granny is not the one who gets nervous so easily, and until today she has never called like that. In his anxiousness, he forcibly left for Hyderabad.

Also on the flight, he was perplexed as to why Granny had called so urgently. Lost in deep speculation, his eyes missed the newspapers that were kept just in front of him. Babar sahab was even more amazed when *jamaat* people came to receive him at the airport. He thought, 'I always come and go. What has happened that *jamaat* people have come to receive me today?' Everything was happening hand in hand as Babar Sahab's suspicion and curiosity increased. But accidentally, when he was heading toward home, a man said, 'I am very sorry to read today's newspaper.' He also said, "*inna lillahi wa inna elayhi ragoun*," as we Muslims say on someone's death.

After reaching home, the *jamat* people preached about patience and death and left. Granny was frequently doing ablutions to hide her tears and searching for ways to tell Babar sahab the sad news. Granny bit off more than she could chew from the beginning. Babar sahab sat and began to call his children. He called his eldest son, and the elder one and the rest were in front of him. When he didn't find Uncle Raza, he recalled, *'Arey Bablu ke khel chalre the, isku kya hua ki'* (Bablu was busy in his games recently; it may be that something has happened to him). He didn't ask anything and reacted normally. 'Come on! Let's have food. Come on! Get up.' He was trying to divert his grief. But he only asked his mother - in-law, 'Where did the funeral ceremony happen? Where is Ahmed buried?' His mother-in-law suddenly burst out crying. Babar sahab consoled her, saying, 'He was the beloved servant of God, so he was taken back.'

Babar sahab knew that it was a major sin to mourn for the dead one for more than three days. Also, the tears which are shed for the dead one will do nothing but cause harm to the soul of the dead one. Hence, he tried hard to remain calm and console others. But the tears which do not flow from the eyes are fell on the heart. Babar sahab suffered from a nervous breakdown. The doctor checked him and suggested that everyone make sure he is kept away from everything that gives him stress. His state of mind remained numb and constant for 4-5 days. After a rest of fifteen days, he left for Delhi, and Granny accompanied him. Whenever any of the family members used to see a tall lad with a pointed nose and dark complexion, they would miss Bablu uncle. Bablu uncle was a part of the happiness of only his eldest sister's marriage. Well, like we are born, death is also an involuntary reality that puts an end to all the happiness's and sorrows of one's life.

Faith Welcomes Hardships but Reaps Eternal Light

The state of meloncholy soon diminishes as people leave their sorrows on the trust of time for healing. The feeling of dismay had reduced by the time, and now my grandparents were mentally stable to think about their other children. Babar sahab and Granny started to search for the brides and grooms for their children, and marriages commenced one after the other. On every wedding, poor Babar sahab would only ask 'How much loan shall I take?' He used to ask for loans from the centre and clear them in small amounts. He had to take a loan because firstly his salary was not adequate and secondly he used to work on a contract basis. He never had a government job to get any benefits.

Babar sahab shifted to a two-storied building when he was done with the marriages of two daughters and one son, i.e., my father. I remember when I was two, I fell from that building and Babar sahab made intentions for me. He intends to go with the *jamaat* (congregation) when I return home safe & sound. All praises to God that he answered the supplications of my dear parents and others, and I healthfully returned home after left frontal brain surgery. On the same day itself, Babar sahab decided Now I will go to the congregation.' 'Why now? She has just come,' Granny interrupted. Babar sahab straightforwardly said, 'No, I can't be late. I intended to do so.' As Babar sahab was working in Gachibowli, the following day, granny asked, 'Your field?' 'I gave some rest to the boys, so on Monday I will make them practice more,' he added. While he was hurriedly having his breakfast, the car also arrived to pick him. He asked his wife *'Accha sa paan lagakar khilado?'* (make me a good mouth refresher). And then left.

Babar sahab used to always control his anger whenever he was angry. As expressing anger on someone is prohibited in Islam, he used to suppress this bad emotion inside, which was badly affecting his body. He was even careless about his diet. All these causes led him to suffer from a stomach ulcer. So, in congregation while he was sitting in the session of practising the Quran, he suffered with haematemesis (blood vomiting). He was straightaway taken to NIMS hospital at Hyderabad. In a while, his family, relatives, well-wishers, and friends all gathered to support.

Specialists were called from Delhi and Chennai for the proper treatment. Babar sahab was in shortage of blood. To arrange for a suitable match, they declared through the media for blood donation. People from Secunderabad, Bularam, and everyone donated blood. Personal interest taken by Mr L.V Subramanyam, vice - chairman and managing director of SAAP, could not be neglected. As always, there was a big financial issue even for his treatment. My father, with his uncle and Babar sahab's friend, went to Lal Bahadur stadium and informed about the current situation. They immediately handed over a sum of forty thousand rupees to my father and assured him that they would take care of all other things.

Babar sahab suffered from critical complications of a stomach ulcer and was eventually placed on the ventilator for nearly seven days after undergoing surgery. When on the ventilator, his beard became a hindrance to the machine. A lot of discussion among the family members and men of Islamic learning prompted the decision to remove the three-decade-old flowing silver beard.

Technically, no matter how much a doctor tries to save the one who has life and chances to recover, the giver of health and wellness is God alone. Each one of us will die based on our deeds and the way we lived. I recollect a small anecdote at this point in time. On one torrid summer afternoon in Okhla, Delhi, Babar sahab had just returned home from Nizamuddin Markaz. As always, he would have eaten the kebabs and other savoury food outside. Perhaps he felt uneasy and started to vomit. In a short while, he also suffered from diarrhoea.

My grandmother confidently stated that it was food poisoning because she was familiar with her husband's eating habits. Later, when he was desperately trying to reach the washroom, he collapsed. Right then, my granny's sisters grabbed him and took him to the *charpai* (wooden cot).

He was sweating. Babar sahab's mother was worriedly roaming around the *charpai* and praying, 'Oh God, give me all the pains of my child. Take me up, but please bless my son's health.' When Babar sahab was feeling the pain terribly and was twitching and tossing, he cried, 'O God! Whenever you want to give me death, let me die on your path.' As soon as he prayed, he started to feel better the very next moment. He realised that his prayer was accepted and always used to say it to everyone. When one prays to God for something, God creates consequences for that person to reach their goal. Babar sahab used to always say with intense earnestness that *'Ghar ke andar beemar hokar marna, ye koi maut hai. Deen ke kaam ke liye jaana ho, seekhna seekhana ho toh Allah ke raaste main marne wale ko shaheed kehte hain.'* Almighty God answered the frequent prayer of Babar sahab—to die in the way of God—and he died on July 30, 2002, according to his desire. Dying in the way of God, dying by spitting blood from the mouth, and dying of a stomach ailment are the three levels of martyrdom that Babar sahab secured.

Babar Sahab's funeral ceremony was held at his sister-in-law's house, as he didn't have his own house, and his rented apartment was not large enough for any type of gatherings. The whole family was near the funeral, except my youngest uncle. Even though he accepted the reality but still didn't want a scene in his memory which reminds him that his father is no more. Anyways, lieutenant of Raj Reev Centre, met granny and showed his condolences after a few days. He assured that any son of Babar sahab can join the army.

Although Haseeb uncle joined the army very soon but couldn't resist their long. The atmosphere of the army was filled with memories of Babar sahab, which used to remind him of his father. Somehow, the whole family of Babar sahab managed to survive, while Babar sahab is resting in peace, enjoying the fruition of his patience. This story is written not to elevate a certain community, religion or a person but simply written to explain what the faith of a believer should be. Babar Sahab's captivating life story revealed that a person can beautify himself, others, and every aspect of one's life, every relation of one's life and the hereafter by merely not giving up on one's faith.

Epilogue

'A Man of Breeding' anthologizes the life of a very down-to-earth, non- materialistic and uncompromising sports star, whose every branch of life has significance. But the root which has strengthened the entire tree of his life that has grown thick and green, which is worth shading others is:

'Whether it may be in this world or hereafter, if you want to achieve success, you have to leave no stone unturned, make compromises, live with self-control and stick to your aim. No matter how much criticism and failure you face, you will triumph over all hassles if only you are correct and patient.'

In the chronicles of Indian sports, Mohammed Ilyas Babar will remain *'a soul of true dedication'* towards his job, coaching, and I remember him always as a loyal servant of God, who lived like a true believer and died like a *Shaheed* (martyred). The following Urdu couplet by Ghalib wraps up the entire story:

Sur khuru hota hai insaan thokaren khaane ke baad
rang laati hai henna patthar pe pisjane ke baad

(A person becomes successful after facing hardships,
just as henna brings colour only after being ground
on a stone)

Acknowledgements

Words fall short in expressing my heartfelt gratitude to my parents. My mother's prayers strengthened me to overcome the challenges and pursue the dream of publishing this book, while my father gave me the freedom and confidence to make my own decisions. I am deeply thankful to both of them for their constant support.

I am sincerely grateful to my grandmother Mrs Mumtaz Babar, for patiently sharing her knowledge and allowing me to learn so much from her, which greatly enriched this book.

Lastly, I extend my thanks to my grandfather's pupils, my close relatives and my mentors whose valuable inputs and support contributed to this work in their own special ways.

Appendix

(1950-02)

YEAR	ASSIGNMENT	RESULTS
1950-58	Active participation in athletics and coaching.	a) 110m hurdles and high jump champion from 1950-57. b) Participated in national games in 1952, 1955 & 1957.
1958-59	Coach - National Defence Academy, Khadakvasla, Poona, India	-
1959-63	Coach- the Rajputana Rifles Regimental centre, Fatehgarh, U.P, India	**OLYMPIC GAMES (1960)** Rome - Italy Jagmal Singh represented India in the marathon at the age of 42 years

1963-64	Coach- AOC centre, Secunderabad	-
1964-67	Coach- electronic and mechanical engineering center, Trimulcherry, Secunderabad	**ASIAN GAMES (1966)** Bangkok - Thailand a) B.S Barua Gold - 800m Time - 1min:49.4 sec b) Jagan Singh Silver - 4*400m (relay)
1967-70	Coach- the Rajputana Rifles Regimental Centre, cantonment, Delhi, India	**ASIAN GAMES (1970)** Bangkok - Thailand a) Shri Ram Singh Silver - 800m Time - 1min:48.3 sec **COMMONWEALTH GAMES (1970):** Edinburgh - Scotland Jagbir Singh represented India in the marathon **INTERNATIONAL ATHLETIC MEET** Ceylon - a) Shri Ram Singh Gold - 800m

		b) Ratan Singh Gold - pole vault Singapore- c) Shri Ram Singh Gold - 800m
1971-72	Coach- the Rajputana Rifles Regimental Centre, cantonment, Delhi, India	**PRE-OLYMPIC GAMES (1971)** Munich - West Germany a) Shri Ram Singh Gold - 800m **OLYMPIC GAMES (1972)** Munich - West Germany a) Shri Ram Singh represented India in the 800m.
1973-74	Coach- the Rajputana Rifles Regimental Centre, Delhi, India	**ASIAN GAMES (1974)** Iran - Tehran a) Shri Ram Singh Gold - 800m Time - 1min:47.7sec Silver - 800m (relay) b) Shivanth Singh Gold - 500m Time - 14min:22.6sec Silver - 10,000m

1975	Coach, the Rajputana Rifles Regimental Centre, Delhi, India	**INTERNATIONAL ATHLETICS MEET** Moscow a) Shri Ram SINGH Gold - 800m
1976-77	National athletic camp at Patiala for the Olympic Games Montreal, Canada	**ASIAN ATHLETIC CHAMPIONSHIP** Seoul - South Korea a) Shri Ram Singh Gold - 400m, 800, (relay) b) Shivanth Singh Silver - 5000m 10,000m **OLYMPICS (1976)** Montreal - Canada a) Shri Ram Singh Marathon - 800m 7th in the finals Time - 1min:45.77sec b) Shivanth Singh Marathon finished 11th Time - 2h:16min:22.6sec Shri Ram Singh represented Asia in the World Cup Athletics,

		Düsseldorf, West Germany
1978	Coach, National Institute of Sports, Patiala, India	**ASIAN GAMES (1978)** Bangkok - Thailand a) Shri Ram Singh Gold - 800m Silver- 800m (relay) b) Hakam Singh Gold - 20km (walk) c) Gita Zutshi Gold - 800m Silver - 1500m d) Ratan Singh Bronze - 1500m e) Shivanth Singh 5th in marathon Sardar Singh 8th in marathon
1980-81	Coach – Hyderabad	-
1981-86	Coach - TISCO, Jamshedpur, Bihar	-
1986-96	Coach - the Rajputana Rifles Regimental	-

	Centre, cantonment, Delhi, India	
1996-98	Coach - Sports Authority of India, Bangalore, India	-
1999-02	Coach - Gachibowli Stadium, Hyderabad, India	-

NAME	EVENT	PERFORMANCE
NATIONAL		
Jagamal Singh	10,000m, marathon	1st (national record)
Devi Dayal	Hammer	1st (NR)
Udai Pratap Singh	Pole vault	1st (NR)
Tarlok Singh	10,000m, 5000m	1st (NR)
Drig Pal Singh	110m hurdle	1st (NR)
R. Subbish	110m hurdle	1st
Maqbool Ahmed	400m hurdle	1st
Ram Naraynan Singh	10,000m	1st
Sardar Singh	50km walk	1st (NR)
Baj Rang Ram	20km walk	1st
Ratan Singh	10,000m, cross country Pole vault	1st 1st
Dasrath Singh	Cross country	1st
Poonam Singh Ram Narayan	Cross country	1st

Singh	Marathon	1st
Jagbir Singh	Marathon	1st
Dalpat Singh	Marathon	1st
STATE		
Syed Azizuddin Mahmood	Marathon	1st
P.K Mahanand	100m Shot- put	1st 1st (SR)
Bahadur Singh	Discuss throw	1st (SR)
Surjit Singh	1500m	1st (SR)
Meen Vala	100m triple jump	1st 1st (SR)
M.A Qayyum	Long jump	1st
Miss. Nausha Thanwala	400m 100m	1st (SR) 1st (SR)
Miss. Salochana Raghuwan	Javelin High jump	1st (SR) 1st (SR)
ALL-INDIA INTER UNIVERSITY		
Maqbool Ahmed	High jump Shot put	1st (SR) 1st (SR)
B.D Sharma	1500m	1st

	5000m 10,000m	1st 1st (inter-university record)
ALL-INDIA INTER SERVICES ATHLETICS MEET		
Nand Singh	800m	1st
Shri Ram Singh	1500m	1st
B.S Barua	100m	1st
Jagan Singh	200m	1st
Shri Ram Singh	400m	1st
Har Lal Singh	400m	1st
B.S Barua	400m 800m	1st 1st (record)
Shri Ram Singh	800m	1st
Har Lal Singh	1500m	1st
Dasrath Singh	1500m	1st (record)
ShivanthSingh Baj Ram Singh	1500m 3000m steeple chase	1st 1st
Ram Narayan Singh	5000m 10,000m 10,000m	1st (record) 1st (record) 1st

Jagbir Singh	Marathon	1st
Shivanth Singh	50km walk 110m hurdle	1st (record) 1st
Sardar Singh	Marathon	1st
Pirthi Singh	Marathon	1st
Udai Pratap Singh	20km walk	1st
Ratan Singh	400m hurdle	1st
Devi Dayal	High jump Pole vault Pole vault Hammer	1st 1st (record) 1st 1st (record)

Salient Features of Coaching

“During a span of 26 years of coaching and training in track and field athletics ranging from university to international level, I could gain a little experience, evaluate numerous prevailing modern techniques and varied systems which have come into existence and practiced by the renowned world coaches from time to time particularly in the post-war era. For a common onlooker, it looked like modern scientific methods and to me it is a simple method based on common sense driving from the very root of nature. Most of the athletic events are almost based on natural phenomena, easy to understand, and to achieve excellence through the abounding qualities of human endeavor, physiologically & psychologically. To me, nothing is impossible and I was able to achieve success through a few trainees who fared modestly in middle and long distances which incidentally is my forte.

With more concentrated work, a few more avenues could possibly be opened in the years to come while the inherent qualities of a man or woman could be put to the highest test to achieve the so-called impossibilities in the field of sports. It could be termed as elevation to a new-high and then again striving to get more elevation... a process to be carried out from generation to generation as long as human adventure survives.

I advocate moral values in my training strictly and have been endowed to practice it in my pupils with considerable success."

-Mohammed Ilyas Babar